DO WE EVER SEE GRACE?
Noël Greig

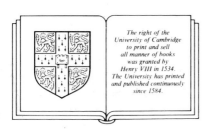

Cambridge University Press

CAMBRIDGE
NEW YORK   NEW ROCHELLE   MELBOURNE   SYDNEY

ACT NOW PLAYS

Series editor: Peter Rowlands
Founding editor: Andrew Bethell

Roots, Rules and Tribulations   Andrew Bethell
Closed Circuit   Mike English
Faust and Furious   Anne Lee
Czechmate   Gerry Docherty and Bill Kinross
Spring Offensive   Ray Speakman and Derek Nicholls
Football Apprentices   David Holman
Gregory's Girl   Bill Forsyth
Vacuees   Bill Martin
Easy on the Relish   Andrew Bethell
Fans   Mike English
Three Minute Heroes   Leslie Stewart
Wednesday's Child   Tony Higgins
The Tree that holds up the Sky   Paul King
The Fourth Year are Animals   Richard Tulloch
Fit for Heroes   Charlie Moritz
Do We Ever See Grace?   Noël Greig
Rainbow's Ending   Noël Greig

Published by the Press Syndicate of the University of Cambridge
The Pitt Building, Trumpington Street, Cambridge CB2 1RP
32 East 57th Street, New York, NY 10022, USA
10 Stamford Road, Oakleigh, Melbourne 3166, Australia

© Cambridge University Press 1989

First published 1989

Printed in Great Britain by
David Green Printers Ltd, Kettering, Northamptonshire

British Library Cataloguing in Publication Data
Greig, Noël
   Do We Ever See Grace? – (Act Now plays).
   I. Title II. Series
   822'.914

US

ISBN 0 521 368995

Caution: All rights whatsoever in this play are strictly reserved and application for performance etc. should be made to Goodwin Associates, 12 Rabbit Row, Kensington Church Street, London W8 4DX. No performance may be given unless a licence has been obtained. The Author states that he actively encourages non-professional productions and Goodwin Associates will therefore be open to negotiate such fees.

Cover photograph be Aedan Kelly.

DO WE EVER SEE GRACE?

Devised by **Noël Greig**
with the **Tricycle Youth Theatre**
The play was first performed in September 1985.

Director	Suzie Gilmour
Assistant Director	Neema Kambona
Designer	Kate Owen
Music	Antonia Couling
Producer	Maureen Simpson

Cast:

Marcus Allen	Jenny Jules
Clive Bennet	Kate Lawton
Patrick Cameron	Patrick McCormack
Reginald Cameron	Catherine Mahoney
Karen Clancy	Patrick Montague
Siavaun Clarke	Fiona O'Donnell
Antonia Couling	Catriona O'Sullivan
Chilo Eribenne	Caroline Powell
Koduo Eshun	Nigel Price
Robert Ewen	Richard Smith
Emma Foxall	Sonia Stewart
James George	Hubert Thompson

CHARACTERS

All the characters, apart from the two GRACES and DRAKE, have basic clown-type costumes. To these they add items to indicate the different types of clown-characters they are playing at each point during the show.

YOUNG GRACE	A young woman in a tatty, tinselly tutu
OLD GRACE	Her older self, dressed in layers of cast-off clothes and carrying plastic bags, etc
COMIC	A vulgar seaside comedian
CARROT CLOWN	A circus-ring clown with a carrot on a stick
DRAKE	A young man in naval uniform
ROMANTIC CLOWNS (A–D)	Fussily dressed in pink and blue with hearts and roses, advertising a version of 'true love'
AUTHORITY CLOWNS (A–R)	Wearing items that indicate authority-status (judges' wigs, police hats, spectacles, mortarboards, etc)
COUNSELLOR CLOWN	The sort of person who sits in offices giving advice and slowly going insane
MR and MRS	Grace's parents, two confused, kindly and bewildered people
DOWN-AND-OUT CLOWNS (A–F)	People who live on the streets
SALVATION ARMY PERSON	Salvation Army person with a tambourine and a cheerful manner

ORDERLY	A person in a white coat who works in an institution for the mentally disturbed
YOUNG WOMEN (1–4)	Inmates of an institution for the mentally disturbed
DOLE-QUEUE CLOWNS	
INTERROGATOR(S)	Mechanical, indifferent voices
CROWD-CONTROL CLOWNS (A–D)	Bossy know-it-alls
PROCESSION CLOWNS	(Non-speaking.) All dressed up like royalty, bigwigs, etc
NARRATOR	Reporter type
REJECTED CLOWNS (A–Z)	No 'character' costume. They speak simply as the actors, describing various people
POLICE CLOWNS (A and B)	
RAPPER and DANCER	Two young black people: street performers. They may have a band of friends with them, who may also take parts of their speeches
CROWD	
SALESPERSON	Very efficient, smart and up-to-the-minute
CONSUMER CLOWNS (A–G)	

A NOTE ON THE DRAMATIC STYLE

The basic presentation is a 'clown-show', in which all but the two GRACES and DRAKE wear clown-style costume (plus any additions necessary for character). The staging and the use of sound and lights can also add to the 'circus' atmosphere. This is intentional, to ensure that the play is not presented as a 'realistic' social documentary. It is meant to create a kaleidoscope of impressions around the central characters of the two GRACES. Even YOUNG GRACE's costume has a flavour of the circus, and so too, perhaps, should those of OLD GRACE and DRAKE.

In the original production there were songs. I have retained these here in this text. What I suggest is that they are used as 'poetic narration' and have indicated who might speak the lines. However, they could be produced in any number of ways: as choral speaking, or distributed individually, or done as adverts or news reports, or even put to music if you have the resources.

STAGE DIRECTIONS

There are two kinds of directions in this playscript. Those in **bold type** provide information that is essential to an understanding of what is happening in the play at that time. For a play-reading, these should be read by a separate reader.

Those in *italic type* are less essential stage directions and offer suggestions to assist with a production of the play on stage.
In a reading they are best not read out as they will hamper the flow of the play, although those who are reading may find that some of these instructions offer help with the interpretation of their lines.

DO WE EVER SEE GRACE?

Circus music, something on a barrel organ, rather jaunty. We are about to see a clown-show.

At the back of the stage sit the two GRACES watching the action. Everyone else wears red noses. Two people walk out and hold a length of rope across the stage. They lay it down very carefully, then exit.

At one end of the rope someone stands with a stick, from which a carrot dangles on a piece of string. This is the CARROT CLOWN.

Everyone else enters in time to the music, from the opposite side of the stage. One by one they make to cross the rope, some nervous, some confident, etc. Some of them manage the crossing successfully. When they do this, the two GRACES applaud. Some are not successful and fall to either side of the rope, where they lie still on the ground. The two GRACES cover their eyes when this happens. Only a couple of people actually make it to the other side.

The final person to make the attempt is the COMIC.

COMIC (*After looking at the rope*) I've got the whole thing worked out. Using the equivalent variants of mathematical calculus and accounting for the sway factor inherent in all tightropes, I think the best way to cross to the other side is to run quickly and not to look down. That way there's no incentive to fall and break your neck.

Mind you, if you don't look down you won't be able to tell what lies in front of you and you might trip over something. So I'll have to look down and take my chances with the rest of them. OK. I've got it sussed.

Right ... I'll count to three and then run for it ... one ... two ...

(*Pulls back, as if deciding to wait a moment before walking the rope.*)

When I was seven or eight, I went to see the Moscow State Circus at the Wembley Empire Pool, as it was still known then. There was a clown in it by the name of Oleg Popov and he did a speciality act with a tightrope. He'd balance a pillow on the rope and then lie down on it, pretending that it was a hammock. He set it swinging so fast that I thought he'd fall off, but he never did. I saw the show three times. If he can do it, then so can I.

Yes, but his rope was only three feet off the ground. This must be a good fifty or so. I'll try again. After all, what have I got to lose? One ... two ...

(*Pulls back again, obviously playing for time.*)

When I was about ten I went to see Gerry Cottle's circus. By that age I was beginning to tire of all those amazing stunts. They made it look so easy it took all the excitement out of it. The tightrope walkers went across the wire on bicycles, carrying little umbrellas to help them balance. One of them pretended to slip and my heart jumped into my mouth. But they were faking it, so I lost interest in the act. Anybody can do that, I thought.

Yes, but at least they had a safety net just in case. Oh well, might as well give it a go. Deep breath ...

(*Gets ready to run, then relaxes.*)

What the hell, I'll try again tomorrow.

(COMIC **goes**.)

CARROT The fact of the matter is, we want our children to grow
CLOWN   tall. But we want some to grow taller than others. Those
who cannot pull themselves up by their bootstraps have
no right to complain, to whinge or to whine, to come
running to the government for help. There is no safety
net in this circus!

(YOUNG GRACE **goes and stands at the edge of the rope
and looks at the** CARROT CLOWN, **who speaks to her.**)

Your parents came from the pampered generation. Cod-
liver oil and concentrated orange juice on the State, everything found and provided, no questions asked. Well it's
different now, it's sink or swim now. But look at the
rewards. Look what a judge and a general earn. Isn't that
something worth working for?

(YOUNG GRACE *looks around nervously. Everyone on stage looks at
her.*)

SONG   (*This song is spoken or sung by the whole cast, circling* YOUNG
GRACE.)

This is the story of Grace
Grace came to London way-back-when
On a train from the North of England.

This is the story of Grace,
Grace fell down and never got up
When she caught the train to London.

Grace was a girl who wanted to go far,
She imagined she'd join the circus.
Grace was a girl who wanted to fly,
She imagined she would walk the high-wire.

But Grace fell down
When she hit the town
There wasn't a net to save her
She was out of money
And short on luck
And London isn't the kind of place
To lend a hand to a girl like Grace.

This is the story of Grace,
She came to London way-back-when
On a train from the North of England.

(**At the end of the song, YOUNG GRACE runs out onto the centre of the rope, wobbles and falls. OLD GRACE shuffles forward just in time to catch her in her arms. They form a tableau (pièta) in this position. YOUNG GRACE has her eyes closed. OLD GRACE watches.**

DRAKE enters on the opposite side to the CARROT CLOWN. He wears his naval uniform. He walks across the tightrope carefully. OLD GRACE watches him. YOUNG GRACE does not open her eyes, but speaks.)

YOUNG GRACE	Drake...
DRAKE	Scram.
YOUNG GRACE	Drake, what'll we play today?
DRAKE	Piss off, Grace.
YOUNG GRACE	Don't you want to play?
DRAKE	There's the enemy over there.
YOUNG GRACE	Where?
DRAKE	Never you mind.
YOUNG GRACE	Are you playing at war?
DRAKE	I'm not playing.
YOUNG GRACE	Can I play?
DRAKE	This is serious stuff.
YOUNG GRACE	I'll be serious.

DRAKE   You're a girl, piss off.

YOUNG GRACE   Where are you going?

DRAKE   Somewhere. Off the edge of the map.

YOUNG GRACE   Where's that?

DRAKE   South Atlantic.

(*He has reached the end of the rope. The* CARROT CLOWN *shakes his hand.*)

CARROT CLOWN   You'll come back with a medal.

DRAKE   Get a good job then won't I?

CARROT CLOWN   We won't ignore a hero.

DRAKE   (*To* YOUNG GRACE) Hear that, Grace? Sailing off across the silver sea, that's me.

(**DRAKE and the** CARROT CLOWN **go.** YOUNG GRACE **jumps up and attemps to follow** DRAKE.)

YOUNG GRACE   I'll come too! Drake! I'll come!

OLD GRACE   He's only off to kill some other men.

YOUNG GRACE   It's boring here at home. Let me come too!

OLD GRACE   Brotherhood, they call it. Then they put on their uniforms to go out and rip the flesh off each other.

(YOUNG GRACE **has not heard** OLD GRACE, **who now speaks out, to us.**)

I wish she could hear me. But how can you speak to yourself? I don't regret anything in my life, but it would have been good to have heard my older voice in my younger years. In those days, all I heard were the voices of liars and fools.

(**Four** CLOWNS **enter. These are the** ROMANTIC CLOWNS (A–D) **dressed in pink and blue with hearts and roses all over them. They take up the rope and wrap it round the two** GRACES, **so that their arms are pinned and they are back to back. The** CLOWNS **speak as they wrap the two** GRACES **up.**)

ROMANTIC CLOWN A   And then he came back from the war ...

ROMANTIC CLOWN B   ... with his manly good looks and the medals glinting on his chest.

ROMANTIC CLOWN C   She looked up from the ironing-board ...

ROMANTIC CLOWN D   ... her heart fluttering like a tiny bird ...

ROMANTIC CLOWN A   ... as he swept her into his arms.

ROMANTIC CLOWN B   And she thought, 'This is what I have dreamed of all these years.'

ROMANTIC CLOWN C   Violins ...

ROMANTIC CLOWN D   Rose-petals ...

ROMANTIC CLOWN A   Boxes of chocolates ...

ROMANTIC CLOWN B   A new ironing-board ...

ROMANTIC CLOWN C   A deep-freeze ...

ROMANTIC CLOWN D   A dream-kitchen ...

ALL   (*Going*) Etcetera, etcetera, etcetera ...

Do We Ever See Grace?

(*The two* GRACES *are in their own worlds and do not communicate with each other.*)

YOUNG GRACE When I get grown I want to be ... (*She thinks.*)

OLD GRACE Before I got old I said I'd be ... (*She thinks.*)

YOUNG GRACE Not a nurse ...

OLD GRACE Wasn't a nurse ...

YOUNG GRACE Or a waitress ...

OLD GRACE Didn't want to be waiting ...

YOUNG GRACE Not get stuck behind a counter ...

OLD GRACE Counters were out ...

YOUNG GRACE I want ...

OLD GRACE I wanted ...

YOUNG GRACE Something high up ...

OLD GRACE Up in the air ...

YOUNG GRACE Not high up like a boss or a bully ...

OLD GRACE Or a person giving out rules and orders ...

YOUNG GRACE Not that sort of high ...

OLD GRACE Sort of high that makes people smile ...

YOUNG GRACE Makes them gasp with amazement ...

OLD GRACE Give 'em a laugh ...

YOUNG GRACE	Make them wonder ...
OLD GRACE	How I got there ...
YOUNG GRACE	How I stayed there ...
OLD GRACE	Top of the world ...
YOUNG GRACE	Top of the morning ...
OLD GRACE	Top of the tent ...
BOTH GRACES	Big Top! Join the circus! Me in a tent, at the top, under the canvas roof. On a wire!

(*Their thoughts merge to make up a continuous speech.*)

YOUNG GRACE	A high-wire walker
OLD GRACE	Without a net
BOTH GRACES	Walking on a wire in a Big Top
YOUNG GRACE	Way, way up on a taut line stretched out
OLD GRACE	Tiny toes and a tinsel top
YOUNG GRACE	Little figure balanced, back straight
OLD GRACE	Chin up
YOUNG GRACE	Gliding over space
OLD GRACE	And down below the crowd holds on to its breath
YOUNG GRACE	Not a sigh
OLD GRACE	Not a sneeze
YOUNG GRACE	Not a crisp packet crinkling

BOTH GRACES	No net!
OLD GRACE	Nothing between a broken body on the sand but a thin blue wire beneath my shoes
YOUNG GRACE	Red shoes with sequins
OLD GRACE	And I don't fall
YOUNG GRACE	Ever
OLD GRACE	Never
BOTH GRACES	That's what I { want / wanted } to be!

(We hear the music 'Entry Of The Clowns'. The rest of the cast enter, wearing red noses. But in contrast to the music which is very jolly, they walk solemnly and slowly in a line, eventually forming a circle round the two GRACES. Each side of the circle addresses the GRACE they are facing (side one to OLD GRACE, side two to YOUNG GRACE). These are the AUTHORITY CLOWNS (A–R) and wear hats and items of clothing representing authority figures: teachers, social workers, parents, policemen and policewomen, priests, officials etc.)

AUTHORITY CLOWN A	Now then Grace ...
AUTHORITY CLOWN B	Now then Grace ...
AUTHORITY CLOWN C	I say.
AUTHORITY CLOWN D	I say.
AUTHORITY CLOWN E	I say.

AUTHORITY CLOWN F	This can't go on.
AUTHORITY CLOWN G	Pull yourself together.
AUTHORITY CLOWN H	Shape up.
AUTHORITY CLOWN I	See sense.
AUTHORITY CLOWN J	It's such a shame.
AUTHORITY CLOWN K	This can't carry on.
AUTHORITY CLOWN L	Such a carry-on.
AUTHORITY CLOWN M	Where's your pride?
AUTHORITY CLOWN N	Where's your self-discipline?
AUTHORITY CLOWN O	You're a shambles.
AUTHORITY CLOWN P	You're a sight.
AUTHORITY CLOWN Q	It's so sad.
AUTHORITY CLOWN R	She's bad.
ALL	She must be mad.
AUTHORITY CLOWN A (A BUREAU- CRAT)	(*Looking at* OLD GRACE) Serious problem, sigh, very disturbing social jargon blah blah blah, inner-city blight, getting worse, sigh, of course it's the government blurb blurb blurb, on the other hand these types rely on the blab blab blab, then they turn to us and our department can't just etcetera, all the same something must be done

	mumble mutter sigh, take this one, frown frown, no papers, no documents won't co-operate, very heavy sigh, no name, just says she's Grace.
	(*They all look at* OLD GRACE.)
	Well Grace, what have you got to say for yourself?
AUTHORITY CLOWN B (A SOCIAL WORKER)	(*Looking at* YOUNG GRACE) Dreadful shame, young child, poor parents, end of tether, won't take advice, head in the clouds, feet not on the ground, won't see sense, textbook case quote leading authority chapter page and footnote, blame the music myself cliché cliché cliché, too much freedom, in my day blather blather blather, my advice send her to a gabble gabble gabble, quite ironic when you think she's called Grace.
	(*They all look at* YOUNG GRACE.)
	Well Grace, what have you got to say for yourself?
	(**The two groups look at the GRACES. They say nothing and shaking their heads, take off their red noses and walk away.**
	The two GRACES **wriggle out of the rope and stretch it out between them, holding it out at shoulder-height across the stage.**)
YOUNG GRACE	And here she is! Top of the bill, top of the tree! Grace, graceful, gracious.
OLD GRACE	Walking the wire! Never seen nothing like it, have you?
YOUNG GRACE	Never will. Grace, the last of the tip-top toes on the line.
OLD GRACE	Can't get a thrill like this from a video-machine!
YOUNG GRACE	Live thrills and spills!
	(**The rope is stretched taut between them. For the first time they look at each other.**)

OLD GRACE   Don't I know you from somewhere?

YOUNG GRACE   You've got a familiar look.

OLD GRACE   Haven't I seen you somewhere?

YOUNG GRACE   I think perhaps ...

OLD GRACE   Maybe we ...

YOUNG GRACE   Might we ...

OLD GRACE   Could we ...

(They place the rope on the ground in a line across the stage, between them. We hear some very stately classical music, very gently in the background. They raise their arms to balance themselves, then very slowly they step out along the rope as if balancing high in the air. They begin to move towards each other as the music is heard more clearly. They are very near to each other. They stretch out a hand to each other. Before they are able to touch each other, the music stops abruptly. Four of the AUTHORITY CLOWNS come forward, two to each of the GRACES. They take them each by the arm.)

ALL   Come along, Grace.

(*The two* GRACES *look at the person taking hold of them.*)

AUTHORITY CLOWN C   (*To* YOUNG GRACE) I've come to help you. Your parents have told me all about you. I'm your friend.

AUTHORITY CLOWN D   (*To* OLD GRACE) I'm here to help you. Can't have you out on the streets all night can we? I'm your friend.

(**They lead the two** GRACES **away in opposite directions.**)

YOUNG GRACE   (*Stopping for a moment*) Who's that?

AUTHORITY CLOWN E   Where?

YOUNG GRACE	There. The old one in the coat. The shabby old one.
AUTHORITY CLOWN E	No one. You're seeing things.
OLD GRACE	(*Stopping for a moment*) The young one ... there?
AUTHORITY CLOWN F	Not a soul in sight.
OLD GRACE	In the dress.
AUTHORITY CLOWN F	In your imagination.

(**They lead the two** GRACES **off**.

YOUNG GRACE **faces a person seated (as if at a desk). To one side are** MR **and** MRS, **standing. The seated person is the** COUNSELLOR CLOWN.)

COUNSELLOR CLOWN	How did it begin, Mrs Favour?
MRS	From her cot.
COUNSELLOR CLOWN	Cot, eh?
MRS	Right from the start.
MR	With her rattle.
COUNSELLOR CLOWN	Rattle, eh?
MRS	Up on her cot balancing with a rattle.
COUNSELLOR CLOWN	At such a tender age?
MR	We didn't know how she did it, but do it she did.
MRS	She never fell off, not once.
COUNSELLOR CLOWN	Extraordinary.

MRS   Then when she could toddle she was up on the sideboard giving us heart-attacks.

MR   The mantlepiece.

MRS   The window-sill.

MR   The wardrobe.

MRS   You couldn't let her alone five minutes or she'd be up on something doing a balancing act.

MR   It's been a strain.

MRS   Then it was walls and fences.

MR   Garage roofs.

MRS   Parapets.

MR   Bridges.

MRS   Never touched her homework.

MR   Never normal.

MRS   I begged her to go out and vandalise a telephone box ...

MR   Slash a few tyres ...

MRS   Go shoplifting ...

MR   Anything in the normal line for a kid, that's what we encouraged her to do, but not her, oh no, too good for that sort of thing.

MRS   Then came last Christmas. That put the tin lid on it.

MR   Don't talk to me about Christmas.

MRS   Terrible.

MR   Terrifying.

COUNSELLOR   Tell me.
CLOWN

(They sit and re-enact the story.)

MR   Chicken on the table.

MRS   Crackers ready.

MR   I'm about to say ...

MRS   (*Shrieks*) Grace!

MR   No need to shout dear.

MRS   (*Louder*) Grace!

MR   I'm just about to say it, dear. Then we can tuck in.

MRS   Not the Lord's grace dear. Our Grace, out there. Up there! (*Points*)

MR   (*Looks*) Where?

MRS   On the roof!

MR   Get down off that roof, you'll break your neck!

MRS   Your chicken's getting cold! Come down! There'll be such a mess on the pavement if she falls.

MR   She got her clean underwear on?

YOUNG GRACE   (*To us*) But I didn't go down. I never cared for chicken. It always tasted of fish. I don't mind the taste of fish when it's fish I'm eating, but eating chicken that tastes of fish instead of chicken confuses me. It's because they feed fishmeal to the chickens, that's why they taste so fishy. And it was Christmas and this was my present to myself. I was going to walk right down the street on top of it. House to house, all along the ridge of the roofs. What's a gobful of fishy chicken in comparison to that?

MRS   (*To* COUNSELLOR CLOWN) That's what happened. Spoilt our day completely.

MR   Missed the Royal Speech.

COUNSELLOR CLOWN   Then she fell?

MRS   Well ...

COUNSELLOR CLOWN	She did fall?
MR	She landed.
COUNSELLOR CLOWN	So she fell. It's logical. If you land you must have fallen.

(MR **and** MRS **look around, to make sure no one else is around.**)

MRS	(*Whispers*) Flew.
COUNSELLOR CLOWN	Flew?
MR	(*Whispers*) Floated.
COUNSELLOR CLOWN	Floated?
MRS	It was a lovely sight. She just drifted down.
MR	Like snow.
COUNSELLOR CLOWN	Young girls don't drift and float. Not unless they're going down the aisle in a froth of net to meet their groom, and even then it's only a figure of speech, not a fact. Flying is a fiction and should not be encouraged.
YOUNG GRACE	(*To us*) But I did. It was the logical thing to do. I'd come to the end of the street and there was no point in going back the same way, so down it was. On Christmas Day I stepped off the roof of number 67 Emerald Avenue and came to land, five minutes later, next to an ornamental pond. Now if I'd been stuffed full of fishy chicken I'd have dropped like a lead balloon.
MRS	(*To* COUNSELLOR CLOWN) Yes you're right, how could she have?
MR	Must have been the sherry.
COUNSELLOR CLOWN	So she fell?

MRS	She must have.
COUNSELLOR CLOWN	Whack! Hit the ground?
MR	She should have.
COUNSELLOR CLOWN	Of course.
YOUNG GRACE	(*To* COUNSELLOR CLOWN) They've forgotten. They saw me float but they forgot.
COUNSELLOR CLOWN	Young woman, I am not mad. I am a sane and normal person and as such I recognise that floating is not a quality associated with the human body. Think of gravity, think of Newton getting an apple on his head. Bonk! Ouch! That is what happens when an object travels down from point A to point B. Wham! Bam! Think about bombs. Thud! Crash! Or dead bodies cut down from the gallows. Scrunch!

(**The** COUNSELLOR CLOWN **is becoming more and more over-excited, ending up by climbing on the chair, quite manic.**)

Think what happens when you boot a cat off the sofa. Thwack! Or you shove an elderly person off a motorway bridge. Splat! That's a natural law and you can't change it. Zonk! Bam! Blatt! I think about such things all the time because that is the way things are, so don't come in here with your airy-fairy floating fantasies because it won't wash. Look!

(**Jumps off the chair, landing heavily.**)

Did I float?

(**Jumps on the chair and off again, even more heavily.**)

Did I fly?

(**Again, with a crash.**)

Did I drift?

(Sits mopping at brow, exhausted.)

(*To* YOUNG GRACE) Well, did I?

YOUNG GRACE — Like a snowflake.

COUNSELLOR CLOWN — It's no good, she's completely cuckoo. We'll have to have her put inside for a time.

(A MAN **in a white coat enters and leads** YOUNG GRACE **away.** MR **and** MRS **wave goodbye to her. They all go.**

On the other side of the stage is a huddle of people in filthy, ragged coats. These are the DOWN-AND-OUT CLOWNS (A–F). **A placard with the sign 'Free Soup' is held up. Someone stands on a chair – this is the** SALVATION ARMY PERSON.)

SALVATION ARMY PERSON — Step this way for your free soup!

(**The huddle huddles forward.**)

Not so fast! What do we do before we feed the body?

(**No response.**)

We feed the soul. Tonight's hymn is entitled 'Grace'.

(OLD GRACE **shambles in and joins the back of the huddle. The** SALVATION ARMY PERSON **has a tambourine and begins to bang it. The huddle joins in, in a very ragged manner.**)

DOWN-AND-OUT CLOWNS — (*Singing*) Grace is what the Lord will send
To sinners one and all.
So come to God and get your grace
He'll help you when you fall.

(**Plastic cups of soup are handed out while the** SALVATION ARMY PERSON **gives a sermon.** OLD GRACE **interjects, but is not noticed.**)

SALVATION ARMY PERSON	For Jesus said, 'Where is grace?'
OLD GRACE	(*Holds up hand.*) Here!
SALVATION ARMY PERSON	Can we find grace in worldly wealth?
OLD GRACE	Here!
SALVATION ARMY PERSON	Is grace to be sought in comfortable beds?
OLD GRACE	I'm here!
SALVATION ARMY PERSON	Does a full table mean grace resides there?
OLD GRACE	Over here!
SALVATION ARMY PERSON	What is the value of a roof over our heads if we don't have grace?
OLD GRACE	(*Bawling*) You've got me! I'm over here!
SALVATION ARMY PERSON	Who are you?
OLD GRACE	The one you've been looking for. And this soup's out of a packet!
SALVATION ARMY PERSON	Pardon?
OLD GRACE	This muck, tastes like rancid cardboard. And there's lumps at the bottom of it.
DOWN-AND-OUT CLOWN A	(*Raggedly*) Yeah, lumps ... she's right ... all rancid ...
OLD GRACE	Get better pickings back of Macdonalds.
DOWN-AND-OUT CLOWN B	Yeah, Macdonalds ... better pickings ...
SALVATION ARMY PERSON	(*Getting down off chair*) Now listen here ...

(OLD GRACE *nips up onto the chair.*)

OLD GRACE	For Grace says, where is Jesus?
	Can Jesus give us a good hot dinner?
	Can Jesus give us a comfy bed?
	Can Jesus give us a bit in our pockets?
	Can Jesus give us a roof over our heads?
SALVATION ARMY PERSON	(*Calling out*) Second helpings! (*The* DOWN-AND-OUT CLOWNS *turn and look.*) More soup!
OLD GRACE	Stinking stuff!
DOWN-AND-OUT CLOWN C	All there is.
OLD GRACE	Not fit for a cat.
DOWN-AND-OUT CLOWN D	Nothing else.
OLD GRACE	I'll show you the back of the Ritz. Lots of warm scraps there.
DOWN-AND-OUT CLOWN E	Not tonight ...
OLD GRACE	Better than here.
DOWN-AND-OUT CLOWN F	Another time.

(**They follow SALVATION ARMY PERSON off. The SALVATION ARMY PERSON sings and beats tambourine.**)

SALVATION ARMY PERSON	(*Sings*) Grace is what the Lord will send
	To sinners one and all.
	So come to God and get your grace
	He'll help you when you fall.

(**OLD GRACE is left standing on the chair. She looks around: closes her eyes, holds out her arms, finally jumps. She lands with a thud, opens her eyes, disappointed.**)

OLD GRACE	Once upon a time, I flew.

(She watches as YOUNG GRACE enters, led by an ORDERLY wearing a white coat.)

ORDERLY You'll be safe here.

YOUNG GRACE There's bars at the windows.

ORDERLY To keep you safe.

YOUNG GRACE Locks on the doors.

ORDERLY Keep you sound.

(ORDERLY goes. YOUNG GRACE looks around. Several other YOUNG WOMEN enter. They are also in this place – an institution of some kind. YOUNG GRACE looks at them. One of them (WOMAN 1) has a doll, which is old and ragged. She rocks it and hums a lullaby.)

WOMAN 1 Never wanted it anyway. Never wanted it, you know, but he ... they made me have it. 'Matter of principle,' they said. 'It was the way we brought you up to think.'

WOMAN 2 How much longer do I have to stay here? I'm alright, I'm better now, better than I was. When can I go home? When is my beloved mother going to come and hold my hand? Did she come here yesterday? I can't remember, I can't even remember her. Sometimes I am grateful for that, but then sometimes ...

WOMAN 3 When I was younger I knew nothing about life ... or love. You don't know anything until it's too late, that's where I went wrong, not knowing. My mother tried to help, but she found it difficult to cope with emotions. But I knew what was wrong, I was growing up, if that is wrong. She did love me, but not in the the way I needed.

WOMAN 4 I'm so lonely here and I'm so cold at night. I'm alright during the day, but at night it's so quiet sometimes, you can hear someone crying. It could be laughter, but you can't tell in this place after a while.

WOMAN 1   My baby can't sleep, she cries, I can't stop her. I know it was my fault, but I just can't stop her. I just can't. Before she died, she looked at me with her large hard brown eyes, and I knew I didn't want to let her go, but she left me – I suppose that was my punishment. I didn't cry, at least I don't think I did. I can't remember. I don't want to remember. All I remember is a corpse, all I remember is those eyes.

(WOMAN 1 **hums again, and rocks the doll.** YOUNG GRACE **speaks to her, but she does not appear to hear her.** OLD GRACE **looks on.**)

YOUNG GRACE   I'm getting out. Tonight. You coming? (*Pause*) I'm going to London. Leeds to London.

OLD GRACE   Better not, it might not work out.

YOUNG GRACE   They'll never find us there. (*Pause*) Plenty to do in London.

OLD GRACE   Perhaps not, things might turn out badly.

YOUNG GRACE   What do you say?

(WOMAN 1 **holds up the doll.**)

WOMAN 1   She's dead.

YOUNG GRACE   Lots of life in London. Parades, marches, crowds of people with flags and cheering and waving.

(OLD GRACE **lies down to sleep with her bundles.** YOUNG GRACE **kneels by her and speaks or sings to her older self, very gently.**)

Grace is a shambles
she staggers and ambles
around about London.

She's a den of her own
at the back of a hoarding
at the back of the Tott'nam Court Road,

where she places her plastic bags
lays out her bundles
looks up at the sky and the stars.

Grace is in transit
from Soho to Kilburn
to Camden then back into town;
she's featured in doorways
and porches and alleys;
if you pass her on stairways
when you're going up
it's quite likely
that she's going down.

(The WOMEN are whispering to each other.)

WOMAN 2   You remember Grace?

WOMAN 3   The one who got away?

WOMAN 2   The one who flew.

WOMAN 4   She never!

WOMAN 2   She flew out of the window one night.

WOMAN 4   Windows have got bars on them.

WOMAN 2·   She flew right through them.

WOMAN 3   That's right. Remember her at school, she never had to catch a bus, she just flew there.

WOMAN 4   And she never had to open a window or a door she just flew through.

WOMAN 2   She was an angel, with pink socks and a halo.

WOMAN 3   And pink knickers.

WOMAN 4   How do you know?

WOMAN 3   Saw them when she flew overhead.

WOMAN 2   She was flying to the moon. She flew there and she took a bit of it and brought it back down here and that's how we got cheese in the shops.

WOMAN 1   She was all the colours of the rainbow.

WOMAN 3   I miss her.

WOMAN 4   I loved her.

(ORDERLY **re-appears**.)

ORDERLY   Lights out! No talking! No dreaming!

(OLD GRACE *sits up suddenly*.)

OLD GRACE   Don't stop dreaming about me! I might disappear!

(She rummages around in her bags, pulling out a pile of old newspaper clippings, photos, etc. The WOMEN **who have just been talking of her form a circle around her.)**

WOMEN   (*Speaking or singing to each other*.)

Grace is a picture that's pasted together
all snippings and cuttings
from magazines, papers and wrappings
stuck this way and that.

If you catch her in motion
from Peckham to Chelsea,
she'll show you a snapshot they took
years ago,
don't known where
but it's there
in a faded old print.

(All go. OLD GRACE **is left alone. She holds out the photo for us to see.)**

OLD GRACE   There. Me, my first day in London, taken by a chap in Trafalgar Square. I paid for a bag of nuts for the pigeons, put them in my hands and they flew down and sat in my palms to eat them. (*She holds out her arms, palms up*). Then he took my snap. I'd just arrived. They said there was a parade that day. Some celebration, but I wasn't sure what. London seemed full of lines of people, queues of them, waiting for something.

(**A group of people is standing in the distance. These are the** DOLE-QUEUE CLOWNS. **They cluster together in the shape of something which might have been a queue some hours ago, but which has bulged at the edges through boredom, irritation, and frustration. This shows on the faces.** YOUNG GRACE **is amongst them.**

All look out towards a fixed spot; it could be someone behind a desk, out front. They chew gum, smoke cigarettes, read papers and magazines, tear wrappings off bars of chocolate. At first, this activity is barely noticeable. As the minutes tick by, it increases, becoming quite manic finally.

They stop and look towards the spot. Something is about to happen. Let us imagine that they have heard the magic words 'Next Please'. YOUNG GRACE **quickly detaches herself from the group and runs forward. The** INTERROGATOR'S **lines can be distributed amongst the cast.** YOUNG GRACE **speaks directly out front, to us.**)

YOUNG GRACE	I got off the bus and I'd lost my bag.
INTERROGATOR	So you've lost your ...?
YOUNG GRACE	Not my card, my money. I've not got a card. I came to London to get a card. You can get cards in Leeds but you can't claim there, not after a time, that's what they told me. So I got on a train and then I got on a bus and then I got off it and I'd lost my bag.
INTERROGATOR	What is your ...?

YOUNG GRACE · No address.

INTERROGATOR · You need an address in order to ...

YOUNG GRACE · That's why I'm here, I was coming about the card tomorrow. Tonight I was getting a roof to stay under but the money went with the bag and all I've got is what I'm standing in.

INTERROGATOR · You've come to the wrong ...

YOUNG GRACE · Well where is the right office?

INTERROGATOR · Follow the instructions ...

YOUNG GRACE · Where's that?

INTERROGATOR · Follow the map ...

YOUNG GRACE · How far?

INTERROGATOR · Ask the conductor ...

YOUNG GRACE · I can't get back on a bus, they'll want the fare and there's another bus with my bag in it, I told you.

INTERROGATOR · Think of a number ...

YOUNG GRACE · I can't remember the number. It was red.

INTERROGATOR · That's all for tonight ...
I can't remember the number. It was red.

YOUNG GRACE · But what'll I do tonight? Where'll I go tonight?

INTERROGATOR	I've a home to go to; haven't you ...?
YOUNG GRACE	Well I can't ... no wait ... I know it's late, but ...

(It is clear that the others have departed. YOUNG GRACE stands forlorn at the front of the stage, at a loss as to what to do. OLD GRACE is looking at her newspaper clippings.)

OLD GRACE	Plenty of parades in London, oh everything, anything you like ... royal jobs, dozens of them, big weddings in the abbey ... mayors jobs, all coaches and horses ... military do's, the big brass with their swords and those bananas on their helmets ... important people from over the seas, waving at us.

(Two people run on, pick up the rope, stretch it out waist height across the street, so that YOUNG GRACE is behind it. These are the two CROWD-CONTROL CLOWNS (A & B).)

CROWD-CONTROL CLOWN A	Alright, keep back, don't shove.
CROWD-CONTROL CLOWN B	Don't push, hold your horses, wait your turn.
CROWD-CONTROL CLOWN A	Take it easy.
CROWD-CONTROL CLOWN B	You'll get a good view.
YOUNG GRACE	What's happening?
CROWD-CONTROL CLOWN A	What's happening? You don't know, it's the Big Day.

CROHAM HURST SCHOOL
SOUTH CROYDON

YOUNG GRACE: How big?

CROWD-CONTROL CLOWN A: Bigger'n the last one.

YOUNG GRACE: How big was yesterday?

CROWD-CONTROL CLOWN B: Yesterday? Yesterday wasn't big at all.

YOUNG GRACE: It didn't seem very big at the time.

CROWD-CONTROL CLOWN B: It was nothing in comparison to today. Half the coppers in England have been shipped in to deal with today.

CROWD-CONTROL CLOWN A: Army, too.

CROWD-CONTROL CLOWN B: Oh yes, they need the army these days.

YOUNG GRACE: What for?

CROWD-CONTROL CLOWN A: For the Big Day. Protection of Very Important Personnel.

YOUNG GRACE: A film star?

CROWD-CONTROL CLOWN B: Film star? No ... well...

CROWD CONTROL CLOWN A: Could be film star.

CROWD-CONTROL CLOWN B: Well, could be. Film star what's got married to a prince, maybe.

YOUNG GRACE: Which one?

CROWD-CONTROL CLOWN B: How should I know? Can't keep track of the princes can I?

CROWD-CONTROL CLOWN A: Could be a prince though ...

CROWD-CONTROL CLOWN B: Or a dead Prime Minister ...

CROWD-CONTROL CLOWN A: Yeah, could be the one who won the war ...

CROWD-CONTROL CLOWN B: Which war?

CROWD-CONTROL CLOWN A: How'm I supposed to know which war ...?

CROWD-CONTROL CLOWN B: Could be the big fat one with the cigar, he won a war.

CROWD-CONTROL CLOWN A: Didn't he kick the bucket a few years back?

CROWD-CONTROL CLOWN B: No, that was the king.

CROWD-CONTROL CLOWN A: Which king?

CROWD-
CONTROL
CLOWN B   The one with the tash.

CROWD-
CONTROL
CLOWN A   Here they come ...

YOUNG
GRACE   Which way?

CROWD-
CONTROL
CLOWN B   Don't ask us.

CROWD-
CONTROL
CLOWN A   Here they are ...

(We hear once again the 'Entry of the Clowns'. A procession of people – all wearing red noses – pass in front of the rope. They wave in a regal manner and walk in a stately fashion. These are the PROCESSION CLOWNS. Then they are gone. The music fades.)

YOUNG
GRACE   Is that it?

CROWD-
CONTROL
CLOWN A   All over.

YOUNG
GRACE   Who were they?

CROWD-
CONTROL
CLOWN B   Search me.

YOUNG
GRACE   Where've they gone?

CROWD-
CONTROL
CLOWN A   Home I suppose. Big banquet.

CROWD-
CONTROL
CLOWN B   Which is where I'm headed. Feet up in front of the telly.

CROWD-   What's on?
CONTROL
CLOWN A

CROWD-   Big Parade, of course.
CONTROL
CLOWN B

CROWD-   Of course. Get a better view on the telly.
CONTROL
CLOWN A

CROWD-   (*To* YOUNG GRACE) You'd best be off, too.
CONTROL
CLOWN B

YOUNG   Why?
GRACE

CROWD-   No point sticking round here. There won't be another
CONTROL   Big Day till next week. Besides ...
CLOWN A

CROWD-   Oh yes ...
CONTROL
CLOWN B

YOUNG   What?
GRACE

CROWD-   Nasty characters left alone on the streets at night. Lurking
CONTROL   ...
CLOWN A

CROWD-   You get home.
CONTROL
CLOWN B

YOUNG   I haven't got a ...
GRACE

CROWD-
CONTROL
CLOWN A   Haven't got a ...?

CROWD-   You'd best get one. The coppers don't like people with-
CONTROL   out homes.
CLOWN B

YOUNG   I tried a hostel, but I'd got no money ...
GRACE

CROWD-   You're in a bad way.
CONTROL
CLOWN B

CROWD-   Best be off. Just the rubbish left now.
CONTROL
CLOWN A

(**They go, leaving the rope stretched out across the stage.** YOUNG GRACE **huddles upstage – the opposite side to** OLD GRACE. **The** COMIC **enters again, looks at the rope, looks at us; then, arms held out, walks very confidently across the rope.**)

COMIC   Piece of cake. Don't know what all the fuss was about. Want to know the trick? Fear. Terror. The pure gut-wrenchers. Don't get me wrong, it's not the drop that bothers me, it's what happens to you when you've dropped. Bet you think you end up like a squashed tomato on the pavement, don't you? Splat! Wrong! Fact is, you don't die. Take her, for instance (*points to* YOUNG GRACE), look what happened to her (*points to* OLD GRACE). What a mess, eh? Give me a squashed Guernsey Tom any day. That's why I don't look down these days.

(**Very nimbly trots back across the line.**)

Too scared to look at them. All of them, huddled under the arches, in the doorways. Could be me. You. Nasty thought, isn't it? Here goes again, wheee!

(**Scampers across again.**)

Amazing what a bit of fear can do!

(Goes. The two GRACES get up. They cross to the rope, pick it up and hold it stretched out between them at arms height. WOMAN 1 with the doll enters. Holds the doll, hums the lullaby, then stands the doll on the line, as if it were walking along it. The WOMAN hums gently and walks the doll along the line slowly, continuing throughout the following. NARRATOR enters.)

NARRATOR A 23-year-old former psychiatric patient committed suicide last month. She had been discharged from hospital under the new 'community care' policy, then evicted under the new DHSS regulations concerning board-and-lodgings allowance for the unemployed under 26. After a few days of sleeping rough she threw herself off Waterloo Bridge.

(The WOMAN lets the doll fall.)

WOMAN 1 Baby's dead.

(She goes. The GRACES begin to wrap themselves in the rope, eventually ending up back as at the start. This happens during the following.)

NARRATOR As the government presses ahead with the closure of 30 hospitals, hostels such as Camden's Arlington House (a 'down-and-out' hostel) are fast becoming an alternative dumping-ground for the mentally insecure. At the same time as closing the hospitals, the government is building fourteen new prisons.

(Two people enter. One carries a brush and pan, the other carries a small dustbin. They sweep up the doll and empty it into the dustbin. They and the NARRATOR go.)

YOUNG GRACE Don't know where to go from here.

OLD GRACE No going back now.

YOUNG GRACE (*To* OLD GRACE) It's your fault.

OLD GRACE I wasn't in control.

YOUNG GRACE   I wanted to fly. You stopped me.

OLD GRACE   I couldn't find the circus.

YOUNG GRACE   I don't want anything to do with you. You're old, you're dirty and you're a failure. You ended up a heap of old rags with a bag behind a hoarding. I should have waited for Drake ...

OLD GRACE   Drake?

YOUNG GRACE   You've forgotten ...

OLD GRACE   He went to war ...

YOUNG GRACE   Why did you make me leave Leeds and come to London?

OLD GRACE   You broke out of that place yourself.

YOUNG GRACE   You didn't try hard enough ...

OLD GRACE   I didn't understand the forms, they confused me ...

YOUNG GRACE   You wasted time ...

OLD GRACE   It was better sitting in the park feeding the birds ...

YOUNG GRACE   Feeding yourself on scraps ...

OLD GRACE   Better than selling my body on the streets ...

YOUNG GRACE   Living in doorways ...

OLD GRACE   Better than a rat-trap I couldn't afford.

YOUNG GRACE   Ending up lonely ...

OLD GRACE   Never lonely ...

YOUNG GRACE   Lonely old tramp of a woman. I wanted a tent with tinsel ...

OLD GRACE	Never lonely ...
YOUNG GRACE	No one in your life
OLD GRACE	Lots. Hundreds of us.

(**The rest of the cast enter and talk to** YOUNG GRACE. **These are the** REJECTED CLOWNS (A–Z). **They describe themselves to** YOUNG GRACE.)

REJECTED CLOWN A	Tall black man with a secret smile. He didn't fit in. People looked away.
REJECTED CLOWN B	She stood in the street with lipstick smeared from ear to ear. Talked of revolution and green fields. The shoppers pretended she wasn't there.
REJECTED CLOWN C	He shambled up to ask for a cigarette. They offered him a burnt-out stub and walked away laughing.
REJECTED CLOWN D	She boasted in the pub how she'd been the queen of Holloway gaol. She sat alone.
REJECTED CLOWN E	She smelt whenever she came to ask for the rotten fruit, so they called her smelly chanelle.
REJECTED CLOWN F	Two old men pushed a pram along the street each day, filled with their lives. When they died they were noticed for their absence.
REJECTED CLOWN G	She'd lost the use of her arms, so she pushed her plastic bags along with her feet.
REJECTED CLOWN H	She shouted at the traffic, spat at the dogs, so they crossed to the other side of the street.
REJECTED CLOWN I	She'd been inside, so they kept her out.
REJECTED CLOWN J	She'd been under treatment so they shut their doors.
REJECTED CLOWN K	They didn't belong in the area, so they were moved on.

REJECTED CLOWN L	Her limbs went the wrong way, so their eyes glazed over.
REJECTED CLOWN M	He spoke to himself, so no one spoke to him.
REJECTED CLOWN N	He didn't behave like a man so the men beat him up.
REJECTED CLOWN O	He shone too dark in a white street so he was arrested.
REJECTED CLOWN P	Locked up.
REJECTED CLOWN Q	Shunned.
REJECTED CLOWN R	Shut away.
REJECTED CLOWN S	A shadow.
REJECTED CLOWN T	A fearful form.
REJECTED CLOWN U	Odd.
REJECTED CLOWN V	Oddity.
REJECTED CLOWN W	To be avoided.
REJECTED CLOWN X	Laughed at.
REJECTED CLOWN Y	Spat at.
REJECTED CLOWN Z	Jeered at.
REJECTED CLOWN A	Never seen.

(**During this, the cast have been unwrapping the two GRACES. At the end they are free of the rope.**)

OLD GRACE   See what I mean?

YOUNG GRACE   It took me a long time to see them.

OLD GRACE   You'd got your head in the clouds.

YOUNG GRACE   Like they were invisible.

OLD GRACE   You're invisible now.

YOUNG GRACE   I was going to be a shining star, the crowds gaping up at me ... face in the magazines, name in the gossip colums. I wonder what Drake would say?

ALL   Drake?

YOUNG GRACE   (*Turns on them*) Yes, Drake. Boy I grew up with. He's not a dead-beat. He's a hero. He went to fight for his country. He'll have something to show for his life.

(**Two more** CROWD-CONTROL CLOWNS (C & D) **enter.**)

CROWD-CONTROL CLOWN C   Big Parade! Big Parade!

(**They take the rope and hold it up. The cast are behind it, held back by it, as if straining to get a look at what's coming past. The** CROWD-CONTROL CLOWNS (A & B) **hold the ends of the rope tightly, keeping the crowd back.**)

CROWD-CONTROL CLOWN D   Don't like the look of the crowd today.

CROWD-CONTROL CLOWN C   Nasty looking bunch.

CROWD-CONTROL CLOWN D   Smelly.

CROWD-CONTROL CLOWN C   The class of crowd has definitely been getting worse over the years.

CROWD-CONTROL CLOWN D	We used to have the tourists, didn't we?
CROWD-CONTROL CLOWN C	Oh yes, I liked the tourists.
CROWD-CONTROL CLOWN D	Where were they touring from?
CROWD-CONTROL CLOWN C	Oh, Hungary, the US of A, all over.
CROWD-CONTROL CLOWN D	Where've they gone?
CROWD-CONTROL CLOWN C	They tour to other countries now. But there's going to be another royal birth next month, so I expect they'll start touring here again after that.
CROWD-CONTROL CLOWN D	(*Looking at the crowd*) Sullen bunch, this.
CROWD-CONTROL CLOWN C	Crowd of spongers.
CROWD-CONTROL CLOWN D	Loafers.
CROWD CONTROL CLOWN C	Bet they don't know why they're here.
CROWD-CONTROL CLOWN D	After a free something-or-the-other.
CROWD-CONTROL CLOWN C	Out for trouble.

CROWD-CONTROL CLOWN D	Here it comes ...
CROWD-CONTROL CLOWN C	Big Parade?
CROWD-CONTROL CLOWN D	There's something coming round the corner ...
CROWD-CONTROL CLOWN C	Can't see anything ...
CROWD-CONTROL CLOWN D	There's something happening down the line ...
CROWD-CONTROL CLOWN C	They wearing their tiaras and things?
CROWD-CONTROL CLOWN D	Can't make it out.
CROWD-CONTROL CLOWN C	We'd better get this lot (*nods at crowd*) under control.
CROWD-CONTROL CLOWN D	Righto! (*To crowd*) Okay you lot, we're getting you under control. And just remember, there's a stock of tear-gas and rubber bullets in the van round the corner in case you're thinking of any funny business.
	(They run round the cast with the rope, herding them into a dense group, like sheep in a pen. Then, holding the rope, they look out again.)
CROWD-CONTROL CLOWN C	Parade on its way?
CROWD-CONTROL CLOWN D	There's something going on ...

(RAPPER **and** DANCER **enter. They are two young black people.** *They may be accompanied by others and, if necessary, their monologues can be shared by the group, each person taking particular lines.*)

CROWD-CONTROL CLOWN C   Don't look like royalty to me ...

CROWD-CONTROL CLOWN D   Maybe they're changing their image ...

CROWD-CONTROL CLOWN C   Changing with the times.

CROWD-CONTROL CLOWN D   Right. That's what royalty does. They keep abreast with the times. Once was, they'd chop people's heads off. Now they shop at M & S like the rest of us.

CROWD-CONTROL CLOWN C   (*Looking at* RAPPER *and* DANCER) D'you think they shop at M & S?

CROWD-CONTROL CLOWN D   (*To* RAPPER *and* DANCER) You shop at M & S?

RAPPER   I was eleven years old when I recognised just who holds the power
and ever since then everything
gone sour
give us jobs is my cry
if I had to kiss them's in power
I would rather die
ever since I left school everything
seems worse
I expected to get a job straight away
when I left school but getting a
job was trying to get to the
end of the universe
a rough world awaits me

drugs, violence and unemployment
if I fall into one of these
for me it might be imprisonment
life in the 60s
Martin Luther King was killed
for certain people their
wishes were fulfilled
who are they going to kill next
they have already done away with
Malcolm X
to make things worse the
world leaders are building nuclear
arms again again
if they don't stop the world may
end.

DANCER I've got these white gloves, see.
You can see them, can't you?
White, bright gloves, kid they are, best kid and cut just right.
Seamed white gloves, hand-stitched and smooth. Mother-of-pearl button here ... and here ... silver white mother-of-pearl.
You like them?
Can't see them?
Sure you can. Here they are. My white gloves, shining white gloves.
So...o...o white.
Like my teeth. See. My white teeth.
Like the bits round the edges of my eyes.
All around the edges.
White.
Like my gloves.
I take them off ... I put them on. I take them off ... the only thing ... the only thing ... with white gloves is ...
They get dirty ... well, not dirty but ...
Filthy ...
Get to be not white.
Get to be ... you've got it ... black.

Tut tut, that's bad. Black's for ... well it's not for what white's for. White's for happy things like christenings and weddings. Black's for ... funerals.
Black's for bad things sad things ...
Black as death, black as night, black as the ace of spades, pitch black, black leg, blackballed, black mood, black humour, black comedy, black as hell, blacken her name, black-hearted, black book, blackguard, blacklist, blackout, black market, black sheep.
Good job I've got my white gloves.
When someone tells me things aren't black and white ... I choke them, just a little, with my white gloves ...
Just to let them know ...
What it's like ...
To choke on words ...

(RAPPER **and** DANCER **go**.)
(**Two** POLICE CLOWNS (A & B) **enter**.)

POLICE CLOWN A   That is definitely not royalty.

POLICE CLOWN B   That is undignified behaviour in a public place.

POLICE CLOWN A   An arrestable offence.

POLICE CLOWN B   Shall we arrest?

POLICE CLOWN A   What about this lot?

(They are still holding the rope around the crowd.)

If we make an arrest we'll have to leave this lot to their own devices, and who knows what'll happen then? What if the royalty came round the corner at the very moment we let this lot on the loose?

POLICE CLOWN B   On the other hand we can't allow those two to carry on with their brand of behaviour.

POLICE CLOWN A	They're taking advantage of the fact that we've got our hands tied ...
POLICE CLOWN B	Taking advantage of a free society ...
POLICE CLOWN A	Get back to Russia!
POLICE CLOWN B	Don't come over here!
POLICE CLOWN A	Making trouble!
POLICE CLOWN B	This is a Great Nation.
POLICE CLOWN A	God's on our side!
POLICE CLOWN B	Once great, always great!
POLICE CLOWN A	We won the war!
POLICE CLOWN B	Hang on ...
POLICE CLOWN A	What?
POLICE CLOWN B	Here it is ...
POLICE CLOWN A	Where?
POLICE CLOWN B	In the distance ... Big Parade.
POLICE CLOWN A	Doesn't look very big to me.
POLICE CLOWN B	S'got a uniform ...

POLICE CLOWN A	Yes, but ...
POLICE CLOWN B	S'got a medal ...
POLICE CLOWN A	Yes, but ...
YOUNG GRACE	Drake!
A and B	Who?
YOUNG GRACE	Drake. We grew up together. We played games together. He went off to the South Atlantic, but he wouldn't let me go with him. He'll be ashamed of me now. Look at me. Down among the deadbeats ...

(DRAKE **enters. He is in a wheelchair.** YOUNG GRACE **leans out from inside the rope.**)

Where are your medals Drake?

OLD GRACE	Where are they?
DRAKE	My friend fell first. We'd gone out on the Sheffield to give the dagos a beating. Cheered on by the Sun and bare-breasted women at the dockside. We'd gone to have a high old time on the high seas, to tow the Falklands back to England, come home with medals and glory, rise high in the eyes of our loved ones. My friend fell first and it came quick, too quick for me to catch him as he rolled along the deck, like something blown out on the breath of a circus fire-eater. Then me, toppled down and out of the game. Out of the big match. Back home, not a sight of the Falklands. I still don't know where they are.

(CROWD MEMBERS (A & B) **step forward.**)

CROWD MEMBER A	(*Shouting and pointing*) There they are!
CROWD MEMBER B	Who?

CROWD MEMBER A: Parade!

CROWD MEMBER B: I thought he was it.

CROWD MEMBER A: Him? Yuk! Look at him!

CROWD MEMBER B: Come on!

CROWD MEMBER A: Who's there?

CROWD MEMBER B: Popular people, big names in showbiz. Look at them, all mingled in with dukes and duchesses, Peers of the Realm and ex-bank robbers. I think I can see Mick Jagger ...

CROWD MEMBER A: Bet they're on their way to a concert ...

CROWD MEMBER B: Yeah, big concert to raise some money.

CROWD MEMBER A: Big money.

(CROWD-CONTROL CLOWNS (A & B) **re-appear**.)

CROWD-CONTROL CLOWN B: Hear that: Big money! There's royalty and pop stars collecting cash for the deadbeats of the world and what are you doing? Sponging off the State. Littering up the streets. What are you fit for?

YOUNG GRACE: I wasn't meant to be part of this!

OLD GRACE: You're part of it.

DRAKE: I'm no part of it! I'm a hero!

CROWD-CONTROL CLOWN A: We don't want to see you on the parade. You are not on show today. It's fit bodies and fashion today. You keep away from the public gaze, alright?

CROWD-
CONTROL
CLOWN B   Off we go ...

CROWD-
CONTROL
CLOWN A   (*To crowd*) And just you behave yourselves.

CROWD-
CONTROL
CLOWN B   Tear gas round the corner ...

(They go, dropping the rope. Crowd disperses. The two GRACES go down to DRAKE.)

DRAKE   They're parading the victory now. I'm not allowed. The medals are shining all the way to Saint Paul's but I'm not on show today. The streets are lined with flags and cheering, but the broken bodies and soured minds are not part of the performance.

OLD GRACE   You're invisible now, Drake.

YOUNG
GRACE   So am I.

OLD GRACE   But I'll tell you a secret. Something they don't know ...

YOUNG
GRACE   They think we've got no future ...

OLD GRACE   Tell us we don't exist ...

YOUNG
GRACE   Only see us out of the corner of their eyes ...

OLD GRACE   Pretend we're not there ...

YOUNG
GRACE   Well then ...

OLD GRACE   What can they do to us? We don't own anything, we don't have a home, we don't have money, we don't have work ...

DRAKE   They think we're failures ...

YOUNG GRACE	They think we're inferior ...
OLD GRACE	But what they don't know is, there's more and more like us, living on the edges. They don't notice us because they think we don't matter, but one day they'll look round and they'll know we outnumber them. On the day when they've nothing left to sell, nothing more they can use to make money out of, there we'll be, saying: 'You've no one to sell things to now, we're all out here on the edges and now it's our time to make a different world, a world where buying and selling and fighting in wars and dumping people in the rubbish bin is over ...'

(SALESPERSON **rushes in.**)

SALESPERSON	Not so fast! Don't think we run out of things to sell that easily! We'll always find something to sell, something to make you work for, sweat for, trample each other and cheat for. And here it is, the last, the biggest sell of the lot, the thing that will sell and sell ...
OLD GRACE	What's that?
SALESPERSON	Death!
OLD GRACE	Death? That's the one thing you'll never be able to make money out of ...
SALESPERSON	Want to bet? We started off by privatising the graveyards didn't we? Well, now we're putting a price on the thing itself. You see, convince the public they *have* to buy and they *will* buy! That's progress!

(**Enter a crowd of** CONSUMER CLOWNS.)

Keep in line, no jostling, there's plenty of deaths left, all new on the market.

CONSUMER CLOWNS	(*All together*) Me! Me!
SALESPERSON	(*To* OLD GRACE) See! (*To* CONSUMER CLOWN A) What sort of death would you like to purchase?

CONSUMER CLOWN A	A nice comfy one in a hospital bed.
SALESPERSON	Private health insurance?
CONSUMER CLOWN A	No.
SALESPERSON	Sorry, there's no room in the public wards, you'll have to die at home it's cheaper.
CONSUMER CLOWN B	I haven't got a home.
SALESPERSON	We can sell you a heart attack in the gutter, very cheap ...
CONSUMER CLOWN B	I've a bit in a post-office book ...
SALESPERSON	Then we can do you a slightly better deal – how about a brain-tumour on a park bench?
CONSUMER CLOWN C	I've got a job, what sort of death can I have?
SALESPERSON	What sort of job?
CONSUMER CLOWN C	Light industry.
SALESPERSON	We've a special offer on industrial accidents this week, thanks to the government relaxation of safety measures.
CONSUMER CLOWN D	I fancy a nice romantic death on a couch with roses all around.
SALESPERSON	Saving?
CONSUMER CLOWN D	State pension.
SALESPERSON	Sorry, pensions don't buy romance, but we do a good line in hypothermia, especially if you can't afford the heating bills.
CONSUMER CLOWN E	I want to die on holiday.

Do We Ever See Grace?

SALESPERSON	We can book you a week on the beach at Sellafield, reasonable price.
CONSUMER CLOWN F	I want a spectacular death.
SALESPERSON	We'll arrange for you to be in the High Street on Saturday, there's another juggernaut scheduled to mow down a group-booking.
CONSUMER CLOWN G	Something bigger please, something epic.
SALESPERSON	Have you got stocks and shares?
CONSUMER CLOWN G	Oh yes, I've worked myself to death all my life, and now I'm a rich man and I want a death that shows how important I've been in the world.
SALESPERSON	Invest in nuclear armaments, you'll go out with a bang.
YOUNG GRACE	(*To* CONSUMER CLOWN G) You don't have to die. And if you do, you don't have to buy it. You can die in your own time, when you're good and ready.
CONSUMER CLOWN G	She's mad! Something's only worth something if it's for sale! (**Runs off.**)
	(SALESPERSON **blows a whistle.** POLICE CLOWNS (A & B) **run on.**)
SALESPERSON	Trouble here. Doesn't want to buy death.
POLICE CLOWNS A and B	She's in trouble!!
POLICE CLOWN A	If people stop buying the whole shop will grind to a halt.
DRAKE	I want to die in my own time, too.
POLICE CLOWN B	You! You were offered a good roasting in the service of your country, all for free, all expenses paid by the State and now you come back complaining ...

YOUNG GRACE	He's right. Why should we want to die, just because you put a price tag on it and start to sell it like motorcars or miniskirts.
POLICE CLOWN A	Listen, if buying death's good enough for everyone else, what makes you think you're so superior ...
POLICE CLOWN B	We don't like idealists ...
POLICE CLOWN A	This world is made for realists.
POLICE CLOWN B	And the reality is, death is now a commodity, to be sold, to be bought, so make your choice and cough up.
SALESPERSON	(*To* YOUNG GRACE) Besides, you don't want to end up like her (*nods at* OLD GRACE), do you? What's left for her? Pneumonia on a freezing night in December on a rubbish tip. Get a good death now, while you can still afford it. (*To* CROWD) Hurry, hurry! Nothing is for free in this world! Get your special offer today!
POLICE CLOWN A	There's nothing for free you see ...
POLICE CLOWN B	Has to be worked for ...
SALESPERSON	Paid for ...
POLICE CLOWN A	Competed for ...
POLICE CLOWN B	Fought for ...
SALESPERSON	Law of the jungle! First come, first served ...
SALESPERSON POLICE CLOWNS A & B	} IF YOU'VE GOT THE CASH!
POLICE CLOWN A	And if someone gets in your way ...

POLICE Put the boot in ...
CLOWN B

POLICE In with the elbow ...
CLOWN A

POLICE Out with the tear gas ...
CLOWN B

POLICE Rubber bullets ...
CLOWN A

POLICE Electric shock therapy ...
CLOWN B

POLICE Chemical castration ...
CLOWN A

POLICE Warfare ...
CLOWN B

(**Everyone goes, leaving** DRAKE **and the two** GRACES.)

YOUNG   So many of them.
GRACE

OLD GRACE   More of us, though.

YOUNG   What can we do? We live in the corners, hidden.
GRACE

OLD GRACE   We wait.

YOUNG   For what?
GRACE

OLD GRACE   You look. Watch their faces.

YOUNG   I do look at them, busy shopping, filling up their faces
GRACE   with food, running for trains, buses, laughing over beer,
        shouting in gangs, they're ...

OLD GRACE   Yes?

YOUNG   Dreaming. No, nightmares.
GRACE

OLD GRACE   What?

YOUNG GRACE   They're afraid of ... what they felt ...

OLD GRACE   When?

YOUNG GRACE   When they were children. That's right, they're afraid to show what they imagined then, dreamed then ...

OLD GRACE   Such as?

YOUNG GRACE   Flying ... they all imagined that. But they don't say it or show it now, and if they feel it they keep it hidden. They're only half of themselves. There's the grown half with the plans and the opinions, and then there's the young half.

OLD GRACE   Do you like me now?

YOUNG GRACE   You don't hate yourself, do you?

OLD GRACE   I stopped doing that some time back.

YOUNG GRACE   Then there's nothing to be afraid of.

DRAKE   (*To us*) Down the street, each evening at six, comes a couple of people. She's old and carries her plastic bags. When it's cold winter and her arms go stiff, she shuffles the bags along with her feet. Next to her is a man in a wheelchair, rolling himself along beside her. Every day, every week, every year, same time. Done up with string and worn-out coats. She talks to herself and people smile nervously. She talks to someone else, but you can't see who it is. She looks up in the sky and waves sometimes.

OLD GRACE   What's it like up there?

YOUNG GRACE   Fine, it's really fine.

OLD GRACE   What can you see?

YOUNG GRACE   Oh, there's terrible things happening, some dreadful things ... but there's more of us up here these days.

DRAKE   And sometimes, people stop and look at the old woman gazing up and waving to someone who isn't there. And they imagine ...

(The whole cast slowly moves on stage.)

ALL   (*Gently*) Imagine ... imagine ...

DRAKE   It's them up there, floating and flying, looking down at the world, at the mess of the world.

YOUNG GRACE   We'll all be up here one day, looking down. Then we'll all look at each other and say ...

OLD GRACE   What?

YOUNG GRACE   Not sure yet.

(All except YOUNG GRACE are looking up. YOUNG GRACE holds her arms out as if flying. The whole cast is on stage, but not in a crowd. COMIC enters, starts to teeter across the stage, as if on a rope, arms out, speaks through clenched teeth.)

COMIC   Keep going ... don't look down ... If I don't get that promotion I'll die ... excuse me, I'm in a hurry, get out of the way can't you ... bloody foreigners, coming here, buying up Harrods ... hey you! that's my seat ... yes sir, thank you very much sir, I'm eternally grateful ... WHY ISN'T MY DINNER READY! ... give me a drink, quick, come on ... damn the trains they're always late ... bloody unions ... have to do it all myself, no one to help me, it's not right, they should pass a law ...

(Goes, still muttering.)

THE END

THE MAKING OF THE PLAY

Do We Ever See Grace? was the second play I wrote for the large mix-race group of young people working at the Tricycle Theatre in Kilburn, London. As I knew many of the group from the first project and there was a good rapport going between us, I decided not to start with general workshops, but to begin the process by presenting the group with a short piece of my own writing. This was a poem about a 'bag lady' in London and from this poem we – with director Suzie Gilmour – devised work which began to flesh out the idea of 'society's rejects'. With the input of designer Kate Owen, the notion of a clown-show began to emerge and this seemed an ideal way of creating an image for all those people who are laughed at, mocked and scorned in the world, but who somehow develop (hopefully) a vigorous resistance to injustice. I think the overriding desire was to create a piece that was full of anger and ideas but that was not a grim bit of 'social realism'.

Noël Greig

FOLLOW-UP ACTIVITIES

Casting the play

Many plays offer broad clues as to how a character ought to be cast because the writer has presented the individuals as rounded, three-dimensional people. We are invited to understand them just as we might understand members of our own families or friends. Other plays offer what are often called *social types*. These characters are not *personalities* in the sense that we have just spoken of, but representatives of groups of people. They may be representatives of different jobs, such as nurses or builders; they may be representatives of social classes; they may be representatives of different groups of men or women. The possibilities are endless.

Imagine you have been given the task of casting *Do We Ever See Grace?* Set out below are some of the things that you might like to consider in putting together an audition. Make notes on your decisions. It may be useful to compare your thoughts with the rest of the class.

- What sort of play has Noël Greig written in *Do We Ever See Grace?* Is it a play with rounded characters or social types?
- What clues can you find in the characters' speeches that may

help you to identify what you want for the actor for each part? Obvious examples are gender and age; but what, for instance, will you be looking for in an actor to play old Grace?
- How will you run your audition? What do you want to find out about the people who are interested in being in the production? Will you ask them to read/perform particular speeches from the play? If so, which speeches and why have you chosen them?
- What will be the difference if you have a particular clown played by a female actor or by a male actor? Will this make any difference to how the play might come across to the audience?

There are no right or wrong types of auditions. Some simply work better for different circumstances. Having given this some thought you might like trying to put your audition plan into practice. This may be because you are going to perform the play. It may also be that you have read the play and enjoyed it but are going to take it no further. Experimenting with an audition might be fun and bring up all manner of ideas or problems you had not thought of when you were planning.

Designing the play

How a play looks is no accident. Every last detail on the stage has been put there by someone with some reason in mind. This includes the set, the props, the lighting and the costumes. Some plays are set in a very particular location such as a castle or a battlefield or the interior of someone's front room. Other plays have a vague setting with occasional demands for particular places such as a waiting room or a hospital ward. This sort of play often has a large number of scenes and it would be impossible to have a realistic set for each scene; so the locations have to be hinted at.

The playwright of *Do We Ever See Grace?* offers some ideas in the casting notes about the style of the costumes to be worn. He has suggested that the clown theme should extend to all the characters in some way. This offers endless opportunities for both the detail of the costumes, the set, the props and the lighting. However, do bear in mind that you are free to do anything you like with the design of a play and that you may feel that you want to alter or contrast the ideas that Noël Greig has offered in his writing. Some of your decisions may be limited by the budget available to you, by the space where the play may be performed, by the equipment that is available to you. For instance, it is hopeless planning a lighting rig with ambitious colour changes, strobe effects and gobo (light patterns) shadows if you only have a couple of stage lanterns.

- Read through the play carefully and list the various locations in the scenes of the play. How might you set these? Draw plans that fit the space in which the play may be performed. It may be helpful if you have a birds-eye view sketched first (this is known as a *ground plan*). If you are very ambitious you could do these plans to scale.
- How do you want the play to look? Is the stage going to be cluttered or bare? Will it have a circus atmosphere or change to suit particular scenes? Why have you made the decisions that you have made? There are no right or wrong answers, but you will have ideas that you want to get across and some ways of doing this will achieve your aims better than others. If you enjoy drawing, sketch out the way the set will look to the audience. What materials will you be using? What colours will be present in the set?
- You may, of course, not have a set at all. How will you create dramatic moods on the stage? Will the props compensate or compliment the lack of set? What props will you need? Make a list from a careful read of the play. Will the props be realistic? Or will they be representational?
- Will lighting play a major part in your production? Lighting is both a creative and a technical activity. If you do not have any experience of the technical side of things, put some of your ideas for the play and for particular scenes on paper and find someone who knows about lighting to help you plan what is possible. If you have had technical experience of lighting and know a fresnel from a pebble convex but feel out of your depth with creating lighting moods and plots, then team up with someone who feels happier with the creative side of things. You'll learn a great deal from one another and probably come up with something interesting and practical.

Writing about the play

A play or an improvised drama puts across to its audience all sorts of ideas and values. Some people in the audience will agree with what is being said, others will disagree. Some people may change their minds as a result of having seen a piece of theatre or drama. At the very least, we hope that a play or performance will stimulate some discussion. It may be that you have disagreements with what is said in this play or disagreements with how it is said. Are there scenes missing? Characters who need to be introduced or explored further?

- Write your own scene(s) for the play. Perhaps you feel that we don't know enough about Grace's family life? Or that there are other sorts of *clowns* who have influenced what happened to Grace?
- In the section *The Making of the Play* Noël Greig says: 'The overriding desire was to create a piece that was full of anger and ideas but that was not a grim bit of "social realism".' Do you think he achieves this? In what way does his play escape being realistic? Write a criticism of the play and illustrate your criticisms with examples from the play.
- What do you think the play is about? The playwright has put a number of ideas into the play for the characters to explore and put across to the audience. However, we the readers or the audience might find other threads of ideas in the play which are not fully developed. Write a short essay on what you think the play is about and what you think the solutions to the problems might be. Noël Greig suggests that the play is about society's rejects.
- Grace is the central character of the play and for most of the time we see her as her 'young' and her 'old' selves. Why do you think she is represented like this? What does it do for the play and for our understanding of Grace? Imagine you are Grace. Write a diary for a week as the young person and a week as the old person. What differences are there in her view of her life?

Drama ideas

A very useful way of exploring a script is to improvise around the characters and ideas that are presented. It is always worth asking the question, 'What if?'. What if Grace's life had been different? What if the world was different and the way we treated one another was different? You will doubtless be able to think up all sorts of issues that you want to explore through drama. Here are some starting ideas.

- With a partner work on two contrasting scenes in which Grace comes to see an official about getting help with accommodation. In the first scene imagine that Grace is a happy successful person who has just moved to the city. In the second scene, imagine that Grace has come with her plastic bags and is the Grace that is: 'a shambles / she staggers and ambles / around about London.'
- In a group, have fun working on some clowning ideas that the various sorts of clowns might employ making their entrances and exits. How are you going to get across to the audience the differences between the *Down-and-Out Clowns* and the *Consumer Clowns*?
- Did Grace fly? Perhaps a number of groups might like to work on people's reactions to seeing or hearing about Grace flying. What do they say or think about Grace? What are Grace's reactions to other people's attitudes towards her?
- As a large group, you might like to work on a 'case conference' about Grace, with different people with different perspectives reporting on aspects of her life.
- What is success and what is failure? For each of us this is different. Are we allowed to be different? Is Grace's problem really us rather than her? You might like to improvise around some images of success and failure. Are rich, famous people really successful? And what are their attitudes to those of us who give them their success; who watch their films or their sports; who read their books; who buy their records; who vote them into government?
- *Do We Ever See Grace?* That's the title of the play. What does the playwright mean? Perhaps in groups you could work dramatically with the title of the play. Is what we see outwardly in the woman with the plastic bags the woman Grace? Are we seeing Grace, or the woman with the bags, or things that we believe about the world?